# THE
# Alfred d'Auberge
## PIANO
## COURSE

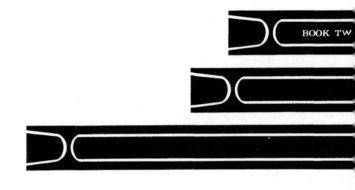

BOOK TW

ALFRED PUBLISHING COMPANY, INC.

designed and illustrated by ERNIE BARTH

# contents

When there are no sharps or flats in the Key Signature, the piece is in the **Key of C Major.**

Key of
**C**
HAND
POSITION

# Lovely Spring

FIRST PHRASE          SECOND PHRASE

Birds fly - ing o - ver, sweet - ly they sing.

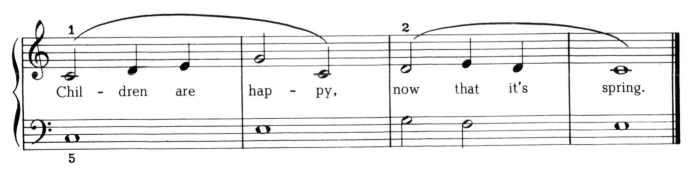

Chil - dren are hap - py, now that it's spring.

When we speak, we make our thoughts clear by stressing certain words, by short pauses, and by the raising and lowering of the voice. In music, we make our musical thoughts clear by the use of **PHRASES.**

A **PHRASE** is a musical sentence. It is a fragment of a melody not complete in itself. In language, it may be compared to a simple sentence, or a line of a poem.

# Music Town

This is how songs are built in our mu-sic town,

three notes down, and a-gain, now go up and down.

It has been said that *architecture* is **FROZEN MUSIC** because it is made up of *related patterns*.

There are *patterns* in **MELODY,** *patterns* in **RHYTHM,** and *patterns* in **HARMONY.**

In this song
we have
the MELODY PATTERN:

the same pattern
one
note higher:

a 2nd pattern,
like the first, but with
a slight variation.

# Beautiful Brown Eyes

Beau - ti - ful, beau - ti - ful brown eyes,

Smil - ing right in - to my heart. But now

where are those beau - ti - ful brown eyes? Why

must we be so far a - part?

# Pirate Clipper

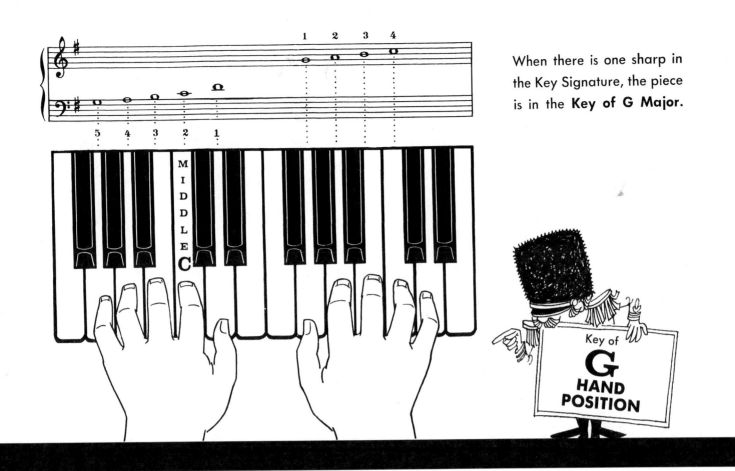

When there is one sharp in the Key Signature, the piece is in the **Key of G Major**.

Key of
**G**
HAND
POSITION

# Mississippi Riverboat

Riv - er - boat is sail - ing, hear the whis - tles blow;

Pad - dle wheels are turn - ing, how I'd love to go!

# Grasshopper Green

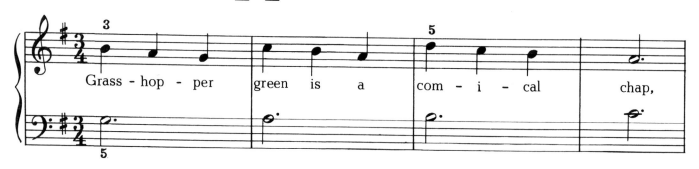

Grass - hop - per green is a com - i - cal chap,

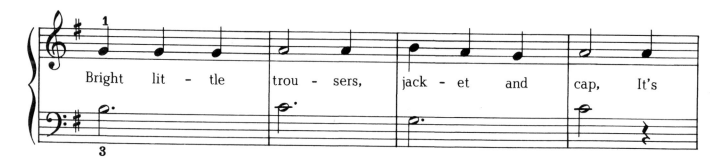

Bright lit - tle trou - sers, jack - et and cap, It's

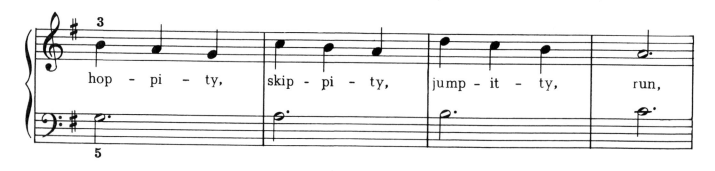

hop - pi - ty, skip - pi - ty, jump - it - ty, run,

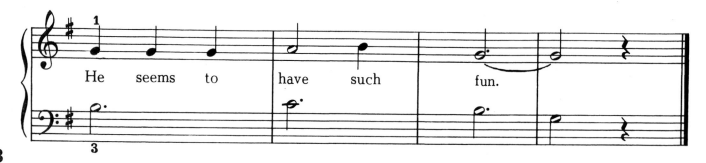

He seems to have such fun.

# Let's Be Gay And Play

Let's be gay and dance and play with ev-'ry girl and boy here. Here's to joy for girl and boy, and for their par-ents too, dear.

9

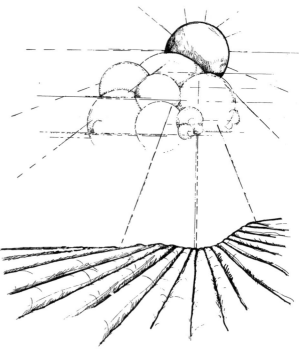

# Old Joe

Slowly

# WRITING RHYTHM

Write the NAMES of the notes in the blocks below.

I ☐ I MISS 1 ☐☐ Y'S PR ☐☐ TI ☐☐ , I NOTICE IT:

I ☐ I MISS 2 ☐☐ Y'S PR ☐☐ TI ☐☐ , MY FRIENDS NOTICE IT:

I ☐ I MISS 3 ☐☐ Y'S PR ☐☐ TI ☐☐ , EVERYONE NOTICES IT!

Add the **BAR LINES** giving each measure the correct number of beats.

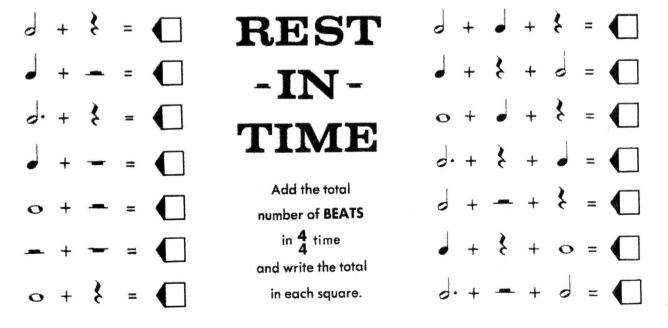

# REST -IN- TIME

Add the total number of **BEATS** in **4/4** time and write the total in each square.

11

When there is one flat in the Key Signature, the piece is in the **Key of F Major**.

Key of
**F**
HAND
POSITION

# The Old Grey Goose

Go tell Aunt Rho - dy, go tell Aunt Rho - dy, Go tell Aunt Rho - dy, the old grey goose is dead.

**12**

# TEMPO SIGNS

**TEMPO** means how *FAST* or *SLOW* a piece is played.

The three *PRINCIPAL SIGNS* are:

**ANDANTE**    **MODERATO**    **ALLEGRO**

(SLOW)    (MODERATELY)    (FAST)

# Flying My Kite

Moderato

Oh what fun it is to fly my blue kite up in the sky,

lift - ed by the wind so high, like a bird that's glid - ing by.

Up and up, and sure - ly soon it will go way up to the moon.

Oh what fun it is to fly my blue kite up in the sky.

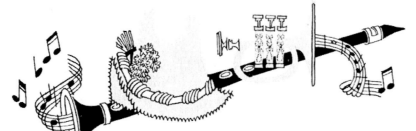

# Little German Band

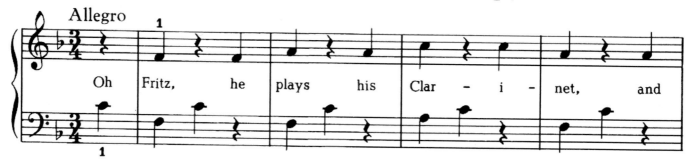

Oh Fritz, he plays his Clar - i - net, and

Wil - lie blows on his old Cor - net. They

play so sweet, and what comes out is

sweet - er than sau - er - kraut.

# Chatterbox

# Two Above And Two Below

**BOTH HANDS IN CLEF**

Allegro

There's two a-bove and two be-low, I must be care-ful where they go, Now

Cross the left hand **OVER** the right.

watch my fin-gers leap and land, like danc-ing tip-toe with each hand.

Db Eb Gb Ab Bb

If we use this key signature you can play this same piece on all **BLACK KEYS**! Play the same notes, but make them all **FLAT**, the next **BLACK KEY** to the left . . . . . . . . . . . . . . .

MIDDLE C

# the DYNAMICS

..are signs showing how **SOFT** or **LOUD** to play the music.

The *PRINCIPAL DYNAMICS* are:

## PIANO • MEZZO-FORTE • FORTE • FORTISSIMO

*p*      *mf*      *f*      *ff*

(SOFT)     (MODERATELY LOUD)     (LOUD)     (VERY LOUD)

# Cuckoo Clock

Allegro

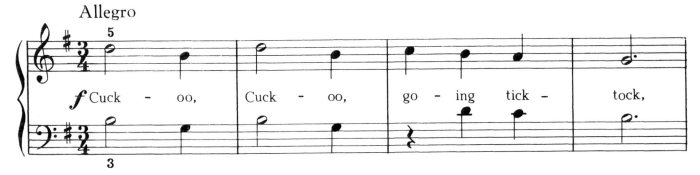

*f* Cuck - oo,    Cuck - oo,    go - ing tick - tock,

*p* What   a   noise   you   make when you   talk;

*mf* You can - not   fly,   nor   Roll   'n'   Rock, You're

*ff* just   a   fun - ny   bird   in   a   clock.

# A Prayer

Andante

Theme from "FINLANDIA"

*p* Fa - ther we thank Thee for the peace - ful night,

and for the love - ly ear - ly morn - ing light,

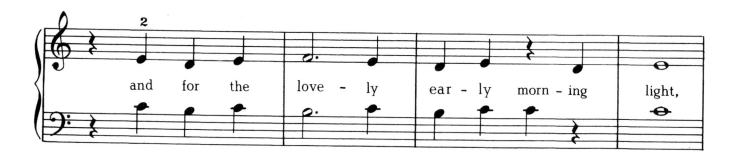

*mf* For rest and food and all Thy lov - ing care,

and all that makes the world so fair.

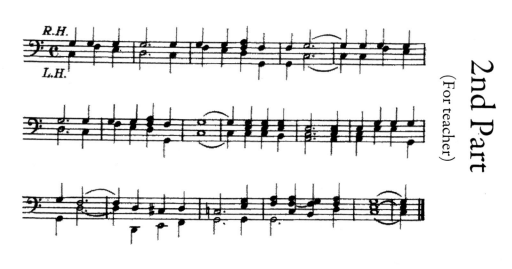

R.H.

L.H.

## 2nd Part
(For teacher)

**18**

# Alpine Song

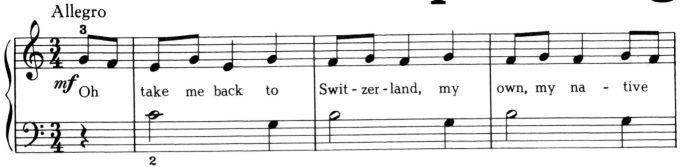

Allegro

mf Oh take me back to Swit - zer - land, my own, my na - tive

land. Up - on the moun - tains let me stand, my own, my Swit - zer - land.

*Fine*

(Yodel)

*D. C. al Fine*

**D.C.**
means go back
to the beginning.

**D.C. al Fine**
means go back to the beginning
and
play to the word
**Fine**.
(END)

*Fine    Da Capo al Fine*

*Fine    Da Capo al Fine*

*Fine    Da Capo al Fine*

*Fine    Da Capo al Fine*

# SHARPS, FLATS and NATURALS

**SHARPS** # **RAISE**...the note to the next BLACK or WHITE KEY to the Right.

**FLATS** ♭ **LOWER**.....the note to the next BLACK or WHITE KEY to the Left.

**NATURALS** ♮ **CANCEL**......a # or ♭ in the Key Signature and affect only their own measure.

The BLACK KEY to the right of C is C#

The BLACK KEY to the left of D is D♭

C# and D♭ will sound the same and are played on the same BLACK KEY. We call them TWIN NOTES.

the **TWIN NOTES**

Draw the correct notes in the blank staves.

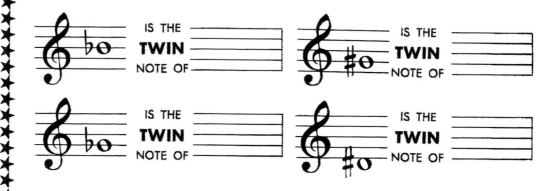

IS THE **TWIN** NOTE OF _____

IS THE **TWIN** NOTE OF _____

IS THE **TWIN** NOTE OF _____

IS THE **TWIN** NOTE OF _____

# WRITING:
## SHARPS, FLATS and NATURALS

Draw a line of **SHARP** signs ♯. Draw one on each line and space of the staff.

Draw a line of **FLAT** signs ♭, one on each line and space.

Draw a line of **NATURAL** signs ♮, one on each line and space.

Write the **NAMES** of the following notes (use S for sharp, F for flat and N for natural).

Draw the **NOTES** given in the blocks below. Do not use the ♮ sign.

| C | C♯ | F | F♯ | G | G♯ | D | D♯ | A | A♯ | E | E♯ | B | B♯ | C♯ | F♯ |

| B | B♭ | E | E♭ | A | A♭ | D | D♭ | G | G♭ | C | C♭ | F | F♭ | B♭ | E♭ |

Draw the given **NOTES**. Use the ♯, ♭ and ♮ signs.

| C♯ | C♮ | F♯ | F♮ | B♭ | B♮ | E♭ | E♮ | G♯ | G♮ | A♭ | A♮ | D♯ | D♭ |

*SHARPS or FLATS not in the signature are called ACCIDENTALS. They affect only their own measure.

# Christmas Song

Moderato

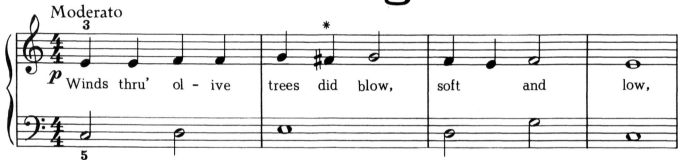

Winds thru' ol - ive trees did blow, soft and low,

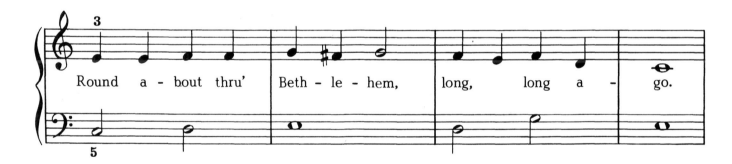

Round a - bout thru' Beth - le - hem, long, long a - go.

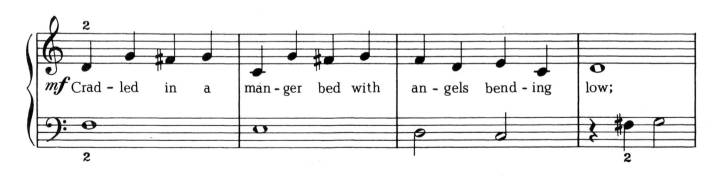

Crad - led in a man - ger bed with an - gels bend - ing low;

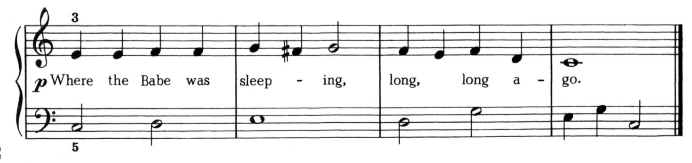

Where the Babe was sleep - ing, long, long a - go.

*NATURALS also cancel accidental sharps or flats for one measure. Sometimes the NATURAL SIGNS are not necessary because the ACCIDENTAL does not affect the following measure. They are reminders and are called COURTESY ACCIDENTALS.

# Maypole Dance

(This > is an ACCENT SIGN, play the note a little louder.)

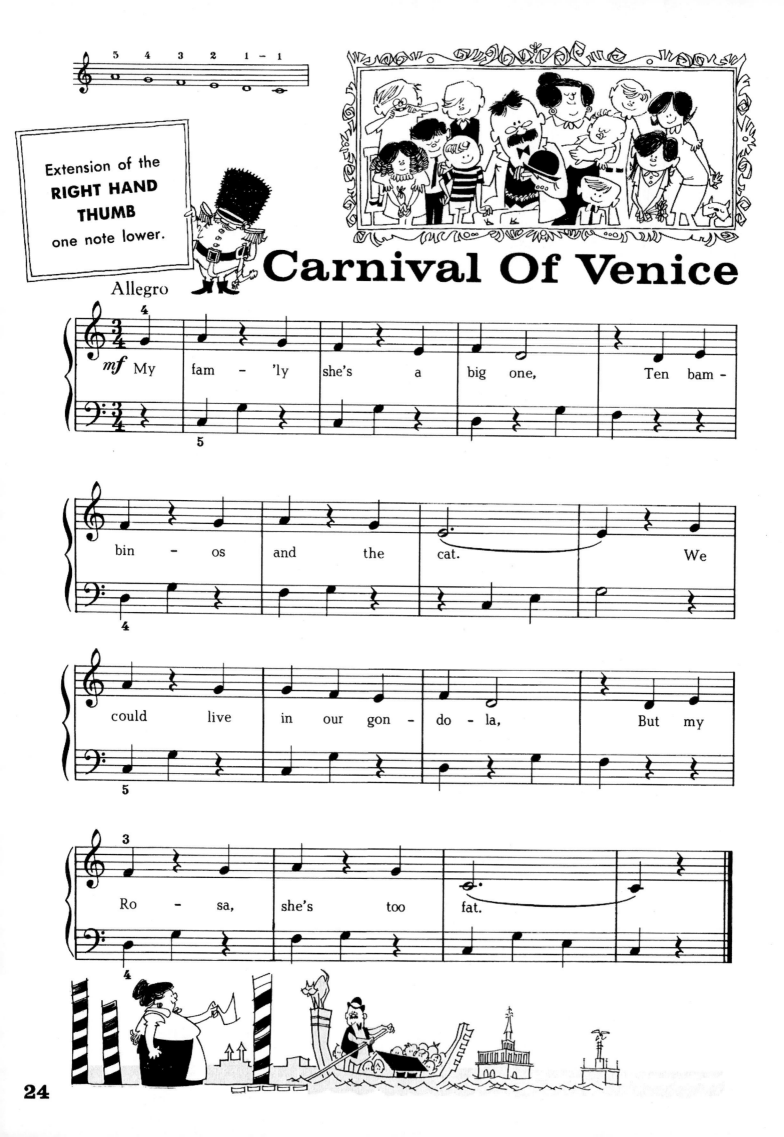

Extension of the **RIGHT HAND THUMB** one note lower.

# Carnival Of Venice

Allegro

*mf* My fam - 'ly she's a big one, Ten bam-

bin - os and the cat. We

could live in our gon - do - la, But my

Ro - sa, she's too fat.

# Au Clair De La Lune

Extension of the **LEFT HAND 5th FINGER** one note lower.

Moderato

By the sil - v'ry moon - light, my good friend Pier - rot,

Lend a pen I pray that I may write a note.

See my can - dle flick - er, I don't have a light,

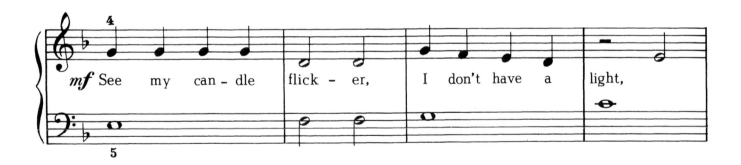

O - pen up your door that I may have it bright.

**Can you sing the FRENCH words?**

Au clair de la lune, mon ami Pierrot,
Prête-moi ta plume pour écrire un mot.
Ma chandelle est morte, Je n'ai plus de feu;
Ouvre-moi ta porte, pour l'amour de Dieu.

25

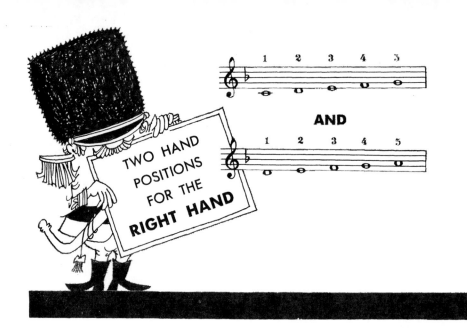

# Aura Lee

Moderato

*mf* Once a young man in the Spring, 'neath a wil - low tree,

*p* joy - ous - ly I heard him sing of his Au - ra Lee.

**NEW HAND POSITION!**

*f* Au - ra Lee! Au - ra Lee! Maid of gold - en hair!

*mf* Sun - shine came a - long with thee and mu - sic filled the air.

26

# STEPS FOR CLEVER FINGERS

**WATCH THE FINGERING!**

**WATCH THE FINGERING!**

FOR A WARM-UP, PLAY THIS PAGE TWICE BEFORE YOUR REGULAR PRACTICE PERIOD.

When
two or more notes
are to be played
with one hand,
they are connected
by the same **STEM**:

(NOT TO BE PLAYED)

**B** BELOW MIDDLE C FOR THE **RIGHT HAND**

# Blue Bird Waltz

Moderato

(MELODY IS IN THE LEFT HAND)

B BELOW MIDDLE C

28

THE SIGN

OR THE WORD **CRESCENDO**,
MEANS
GROW LOUDER.

THE SIGN

OR THE WORD **DIMINUENDO**,
MEANS
GROW SOFTER.

# Echo Waltz

# the ROUND

A ROUND is a simple melody for three or more voices, each voice taking up the melody at different times. It goes back to the 14th century when it was known as a *Roundelay*, or *Roundel*. As a dance, it was a *Circle*, or *Round* dance.

# Lovely Evening

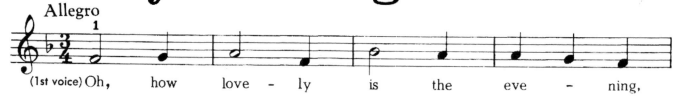

(1st voice) Oh, how love - ly is the eve - ning,

is the eve - ning, When the bells are

(2nd voice) Oh, how love - ly

sweet - ly ring - ing, sweet - ly ring - ing,

is the eve - ning, is the eve - ning,

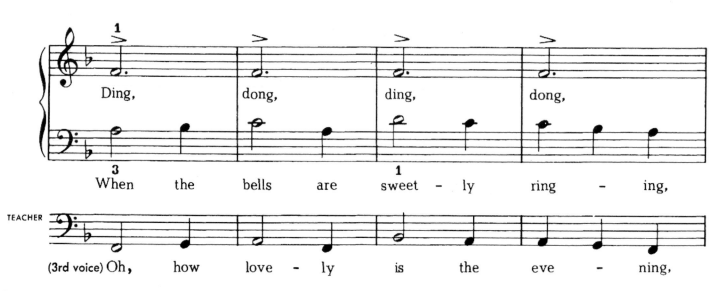

Ding, dong, ding, dong,

When the bells are sweet - ly ring - ing,

TEACHER

(3rd voice) Oh, how love - ly is the eve - ning,

30

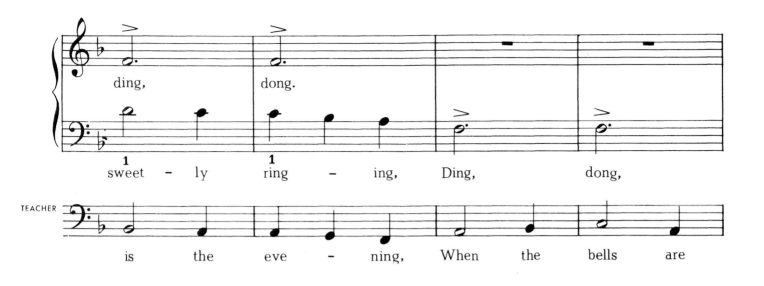

ding, dong.

sweet – ly ring – ing, Ding, dong,

*TEACHER*

is the eve – ning, When the bells are

(Omit RIGHT HAND the 2nd time)

Oh, how love – ly

ding, dong, ding, dong.

*TEACHER*

sweet – ly ring – ing, sweet – ly ring – ing,

is the eve – ning, is the eve – ning,

*TEACHER*

Ding, dong, ding, dong.

# Introducing DOTTED QUARTER NOTES

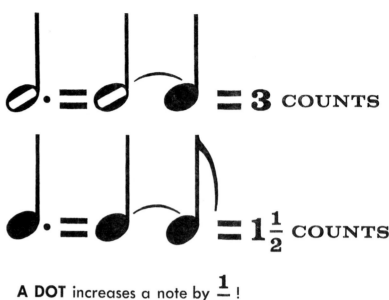

A **DOT** increases a note by $\frac{1}{2}$ !

# PREPARATORY DRILL

The only difference in the following three measures

...and those directly below them is the way they are written. They should sound **the SAME**.

Count:  1    2 and  3  4

# The Road Home

Andante

NEW NOTE FOR **LEFT HAND**

For every Major key, there is a minor key with the same signature called the **RELATIVE MINOR KEY.** The keys of A Minor and C Major are relative keys because they have the same key signature, (no sharps, no flats). Usually the last note of the melody will end on the note of the key.

# The Drum Dance

# The Crafty Crocodile

We learned that A minor is the relative key of C major because they both have the same signature: **NO SHARPS OR FLATS.**

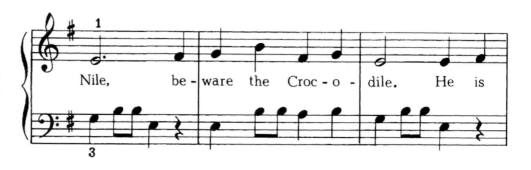

Allegro

*mf*

If you sail the

This piece is in the key of E minor. E minor is the relative minor key of ____ major because they both have the same signature: **ONE SHARP.**

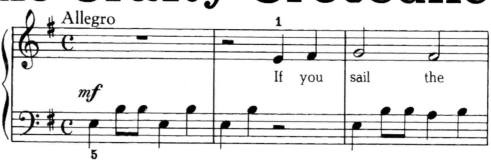

Nile, be - ware the Croc - o - dile. He is

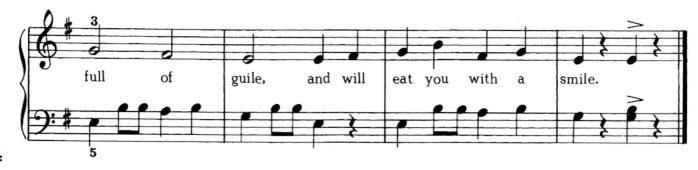

full of guile, and will eat you with a smile.

# MUSICAL CROSSWORD PUZZLE

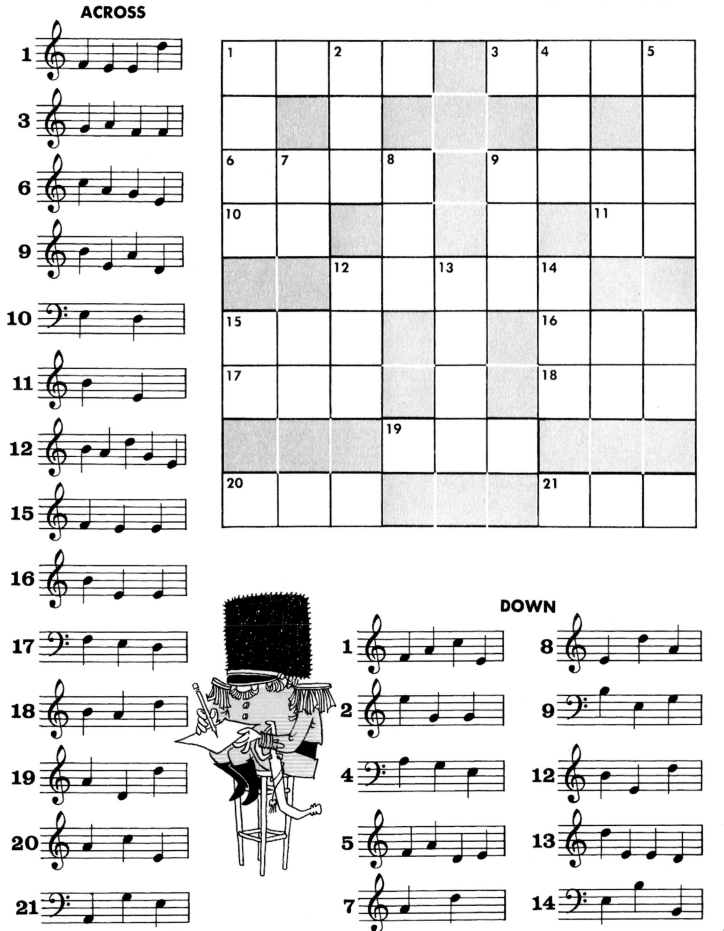

This piece is in the key of D minor.
D minor is the relative minor key of
_____major because they both have
the same signature: **ONE FLAT**.

# Mr. Nobody

Moderato

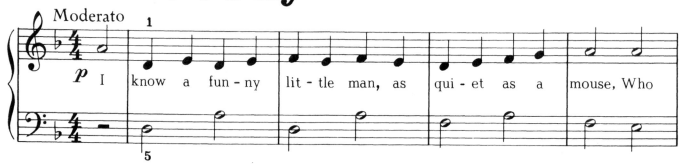

*p* I know a fun-ny lit-tle man, as qui-et as a mouse, Who

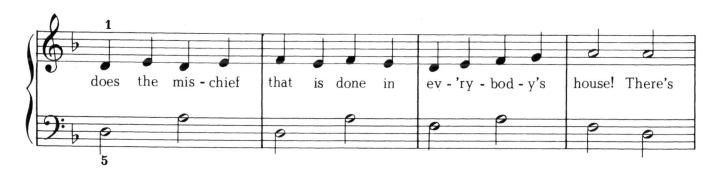

does the mis-chief that is done in ev-'ry-bod-y's house! There's

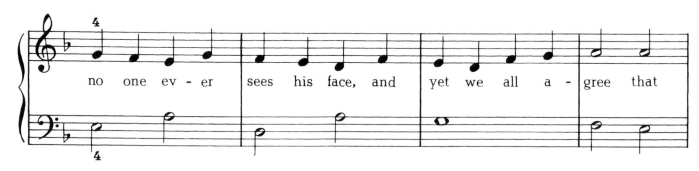

no one ev-er sees his face, and yet we all a-gree that

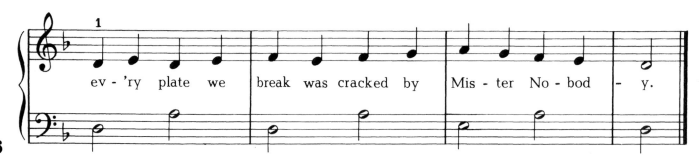

ev-'ry plate we break was cracked by Mis-ter No-bod-y.

# The Old Grey Mare

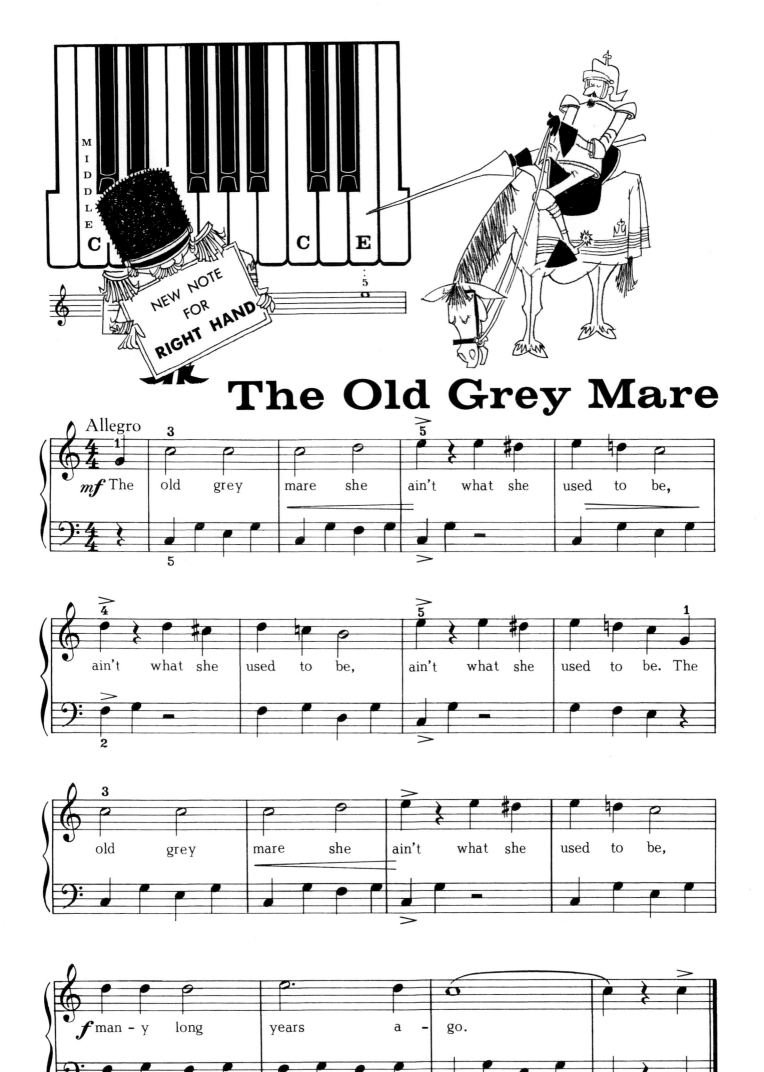

# the MAJOR SCALE

**A SCALE** is a succession of eight tones in alphabetical rotation. All **MAJOR SCALES** are built in the same form:

**WHOLE STEP, WHOLE STEP, HALF STEP;**

**WHOLE STEP, WHOLE STEP, WHOLE STEP, HALF STEP.**

## HALF STEPS•NO KEY BETWEEN

## WHOLE STEPS•ONE KEY BETWEEN

★★★★★★★★★★★★★★★★★★★★★★★★★★★★★★★★★★★★★★★★★★★★★★★★★★★★★

This scale has eight notes. The highest note, having the same letter-name as the first note, is called the • • • • • • • • • • • • • • • • • • • • • • • • • • • • • • • OCTAVE NOTE

# C MAJOR SCALE

When a scale is written with the ½ steps from the 3rd to 4th and 7th to 8th notes of the scale, it is a **MAJOR SCALE**, and is given the name of the first note.

# the ONE-OCTAVE SCALE (FOR TWO HANDS)

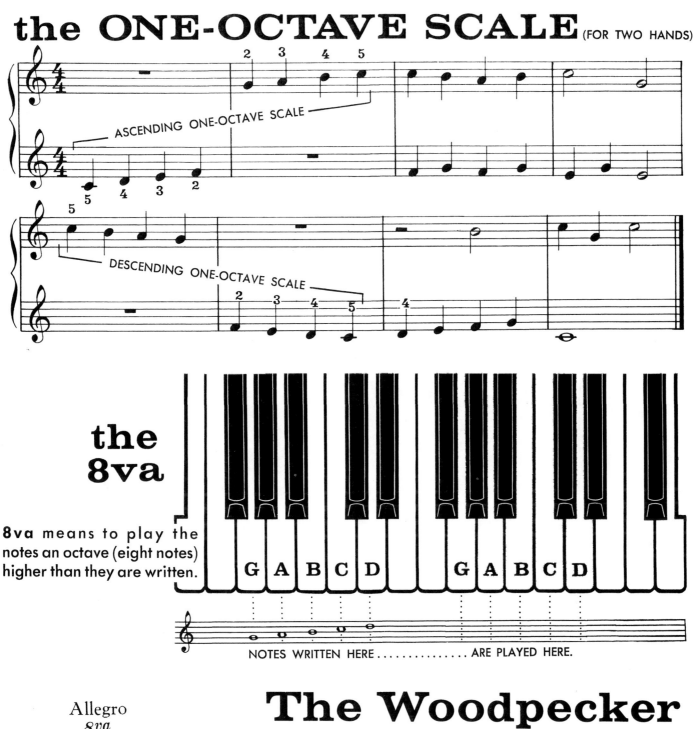

## the 8va

**8va** means to play the notes an octave (eight notes) higher than they are written.

NOTES WRITTEN HERE . . . . . . . . . . . . . . ARE PLAYED HERE.

# The Woodpecker

Allegro

*Loco cancels the 8va.

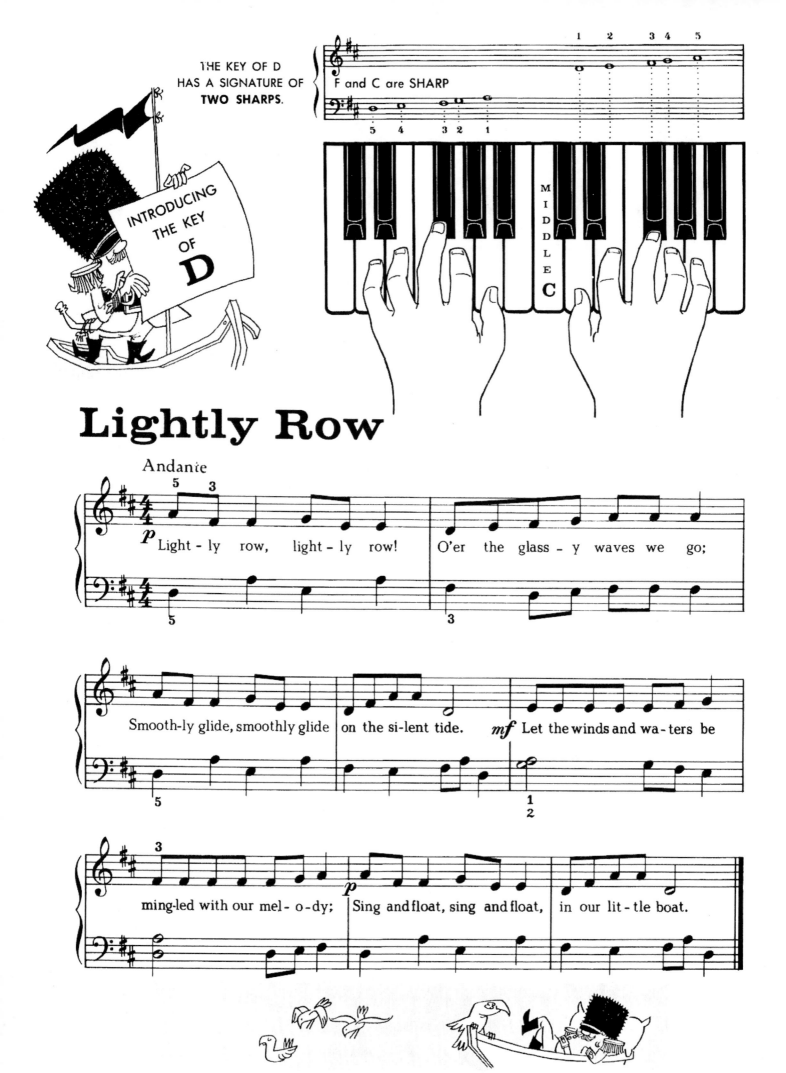

THE KEY OF D
HAS A SIGNATURE OF
**TWO SHARPS.**

F and C are SHARP

# Lightly Row

Andante

Light-ly row, light-ly row! O'er the glass-y waves we go;

Smooth-ly glide, smoothly glide on the si-lent tide. Let the winds and wa-ters be

ming-led with our mel-o-dy; Sing and float, sing and float, in our lit-tle boat.

# The Barefoot Geese

Moderato

*mf* Su - sy, lit - tle Su - sy, now what is the news? The

geese are go - ing bare - foot be - cause they have no shoes, The

cob - bler has leath - er but no last has he,

so he can - not make them shoes, *p* don't you see?

INTRODUCING THE KEY
OF
**B♭**

THE KEY OF B♭ HAS A
SIGNATURE OF **TWO FLATS.**

B and E are **FLAT**

INTRODUCING
LOW
**B**
FOR THE
**LEFT HAND**

B C

MIDDLE C

# A-Tiskit, A-Taskit

Moderato

*mf* A - tis - kit, a - tas - kit, A green and yel - low bas - ket, I

wrote a let - ter to my love and on the way I dropped it, I

dropped it, I dropped it, And on the way I dropped it. A

lit - tle pup - py picked it up And car - ried it a - way.

42

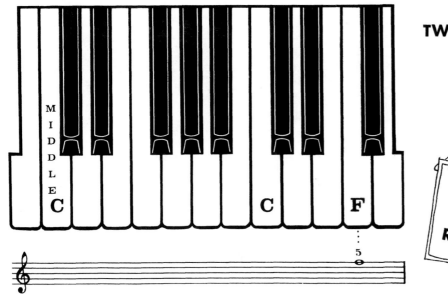

NEW NOTE
FOR
RIGHT HAND

# Skip To My Lou

Allegro

*mf* Come, let's line up, point your shoe! Come, let's line up, point your shoe!

Choose your part-ner, choose me do! Skip to my Lou my dar-ling.

# Now The Day Is Over

Andante

*p* Now the day is o-ver, Night is draw-ing nigh,

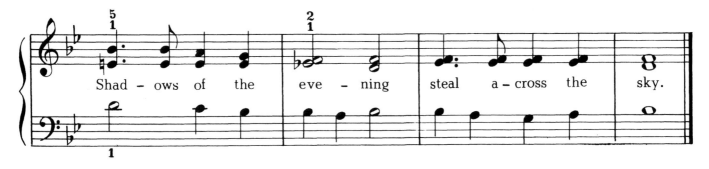

Shad-ows of the eve-ning steal a-cross the sky.

# LEGATO and DETACHED

So far, we have learned the **TIE** that connects notes of the same pitch:

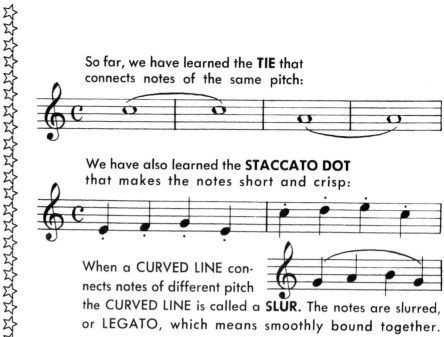

We have also learned the **STACCATO DOT** that makes the notes short and crisp:

When a CURVED LINE connects notes of different pitch the CURVED LINE is called a **SLUR**. The notes are slurred, or LEGATO, which means smoothly bound together.

Play these four notes:

Now hum them without breathing, or stopping between any of the notes. Play them again just as you hummed them and you are playing the notes **LEGATO**.

*Notes that have neither the STACCATO DOT nor the SLUR are said to be DETACHED. Say the letters A, B, C, D. Notice that you do not run them together like a SLUR, nor do you say them short and crisp like the STACCATO. You say them DETACHED. Notes without the SLUR or STACCATO DOT are played **DETACHED**.

# Big Rock Candy Mountain

Moderato

mf On a sum-mer day in the month of May a cow-boy came a - hik-ing, down a

shad - y lane through the su - gar cane he was look-ing for his lik - ing. As he

roamed a - long he sang a song of the land of milk and hon - ey, where a

man can stay for man-y a day and he won't need an - y mon - ey.

# Music Box

Moderato
*8va* THROUGHOUT

# QUIZ

1. A phrase is a musical_____

2. In $\frac{2}{4}$ time there are_____beats in each measure.

3. Tempo means how_____or_____a piece is played.

4. The three principal tempo signs are:_____,_____and_____.

5. The signature of the key of D major is_____.

6. When a scale has eight notes, the highest note is called the_____note.

7. The signs showing whether the music is soft or loud are called_____.

8. 8va means to play the notes_____.

9. The dynamic sign $p$ means_____, $f$ means_____.

10. The signature of the key of B♭ major is_____.

11. The sign ◁ or the word crescendo means_____.

12. Andante means_____. Allegro means_____.

13. Notes that are neither staccato nor slurred are called_____.

14. D.C. al Fine means_____.

15. A # or ♭ not in the key signature is called an_____.

16. D minor is the relative minor key of_____major.

17. The sign ▷ or the word diminuendo means_____.

18. The dynamic sign $mf$ means_____. $ff$ means_____.

19. E minor is the relative minor key of_____major.

20. A scale is a succession of_____tones in_____rotation.

# Certificate of Promotion

This certifies that

_____

has mastered and perfected
Book 2 of the **ALFRED d'AUBERGE PIANO COURSE**
and is hereby promoted into
Book 3 of the **ALFRED d'AUBERGE PIANO COURSE**

Teacher _____

Date _____